D0601392

Who Needs a DESERT?

A Desert Ecosystem

KAREN PATKAU

TUNDRA BOOKS

Published in Canada by Tundra Books, a division of Random House of Canada, One Toronto Street, Suite 300, Toronto, Ontario M5C 2V6

Published in the United States by Tundra Books of Northern New York, P.O. Box 1030, Plattsburgh, New York 12901

Library of Congress Control Number: 2013943890

Library and Archives Canada Cataloguing in Publication

Patkau, Karen, author
  Who needs a desert? : a desert ecosystem / by Karen Patkau.

(Ecosystem series)
Ages 7-10.
Issued in print and electronic formats.
ISBN 978-1-77049-386-5 (bound). – ISBN 978-1-77049-387-2 (epub)

  1. Desert ecology – Juvenile literature. I. Title. II. Series:
Patkau, Karen. Ecosystem series.

QH541.5.D4P38 2014   j577.54   C2013-904502-3
                                             C2013-904503-1

Edited by Sue Tate
Designed by Karen Patkau
The artwork in this book was digitally rendered.

www.tundrabooks.com

Printed and bound in China

1 2 3 4 5 6   19 18 17 16 15 14

To Dr. Jane Berg,

with special thanks to my family and friends.

WELCOME TO THE DESERT

The sun burns in a cloudless sky. Scrubby plants, rocks, and boulders are scattered over hot sandy ground.

"*Yip-yip-awoooo,*" howls a lone coyote. In the distance, another howls back.

A Gila monster finds shelter under a prickly pear cactus. As black vultures soar overhead, a black-tailed jackrabbit barely twitches his ears.

Springwater and rivers are scarce. There is little rain, and the earth dries up quickly after a rare downpour. This harsh, dry place is a desert.

THE DESERT IS DRY LAND

Deserts form when global air movements, driven by the earth's daily rotation and ocean currents, interact with water and landforms. This creates areas of dry or arid land.

Most deserts are found in areas north and south of the equator, which is an imaginary circle around the middle of the earth.

GLOBAL AIR MOVEMENTS

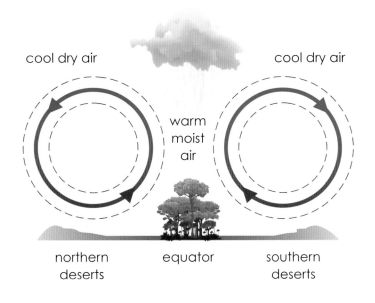

cool dry air

cool dry air

warm
moist
air

northern
deserts

equator

southern
deserts

LIVING IN THE DESERT

Plants and animals have adapted to the severe environment, finding ways to survive within their dry ecosystem. Let's meet more of this desert's inhabitants.

In the fresh morning air, a javelina nibbles on a brittlebush. Sun shines on desert holly. A roadrunner snaps up a giant desert centipede.

Prickly cactus spines lose little moisture from their narrow surfaces. They protect fleshy cactus stems, which soak up and store precious water.

After a busy night, a ringtail *yawwwns* and drifts off to sleep in her den.

By noon, the desert sizzles. A pocket mouse rests comfortably underground in a burrow. His breath keeps the burrow cool and damp.

Quails bolt across an open space to take cover beneath a creosote bush.

The bush's roots reach outward, just below the surface of sandy soil, absorbing any rainwater or dew.

Beside a shady rock, a Harris's antelope squirrel spreads out on the ground. She will not get as thirsty if she stays still.

At dusk, the desert air cools.

A western diamondback rattlesnake slithers out from beneath a shrub. A tarantula feels the ground vibrate in front of his den as the snake passes by.

Curious mountain lion cubs and their mother watch from a distance.

A Gila woodpecker looks down from her hollowed-out nest, high in a saguaro cactus. Her eggs are safe up here.

After the blazing sun disappears, the night air is chilly. As stars sparkle above, a desert tortoise retreats into her burrow for warmth.

The nocturnal creatures are hungry. A bark scorpion scuttles after a spider. An elf owl snatches a silk moth from a branch.

Hopping about, a kangaroo rat collects seeds in her cheek pouches. A kit fox spots her and lunges. *Phew!* She escapes.

Huge saguaro cacti are blooming tonight. Lesser long-nosed bats flap from one to another, lapping up sweet nectar from the flowers and pollinating them.

HOW DESERT SOIL FORMS

Over centuries, weathering and temperature swings between hot days and cold nights break up the desert's rocky surface into sand and gravel.

Sand dunes cover some of the driest areas. In others, dust, stones, and rocks slowly pack down into hard "desert pavement."

On a shady slope, draining rainwater once deposited nutritious soil. Much has eroded. "Desert scrub" – grasses, cacti, shrubs, and trees – grows in what remains.

Mesquite and palo verde trees provide this soil with cover, nutrients, and organic matter. This makes it more moist, cool, and fertile than the soil in direct sunlight.

THE FOOD CHAIN

All plants and animals need energy from food to survive. When this energy passes from one living thing to another to another, it is called a food chain.

Plants make their own food, using water, carbon dioxide from the air, and the sun's energy.

Animals must feed on other living things.

Plant-eaters, such as mule deer, are called herbivores. Meat-eaters, like Harris's hawks, are called carnivores.

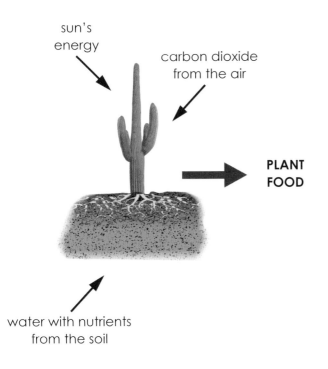

sun's energy

carbon dioxide from the air

PLANT FOOD

water with nutrients from the soil

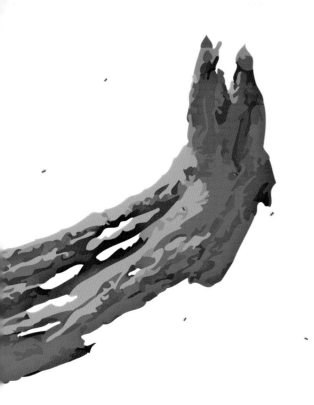

BACTERIA

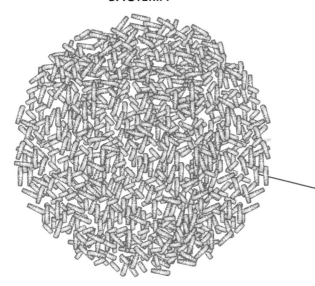

LIFE IS A CYCLE

Someday, all living things die. Animal scavengers eat carcasses and dead plants.

Decomposers, such as bacteria and fungi, live on and break down leftover dead matter.

They turn it into substances necessary to sustain life, including nutrients that plants need to grow.

DESERT RAIN

This desert has two rainy seasons. Winter is usually sunny and mild, but some days bring wind, cold, and rain.

Thunderstorms arrive in summer. Dry valleys become rivers of rainwater. This is the main growing season for trees and shrubs.

When it rains, plants quickly flower and produce seeds. Seeds, sometimes lying in dry soil for years, sprout as soon as they become wet.

Spadefoot toads, buried for months in their burrows, struggle to the surface. Within a day, they gather in puddles, mate, and lay eggs. Tadpoles soon hatch and develop into frogs.

DESERT LAND BECOMES BARREN

Throughout history, small groups of people have lived near deserts – growing crops with water from wells and rivers, or traveling with their grazing animals in search of plants to eat.

As modern people move into desert areas, they irrigate land for farming. The irrigation water evaporates and leaves salt behind. Eventually, plants cannot grow in this salty soil.

Where natural water supplies become drained, land becomes drier. When plants use up the soil's nutrients, they die. The desert cannot support new growth.

Plant roots hold shallow topsoil in place. Without plants, wind carries the soil away. A lifeless land, useless for crops or pastures, remains.

Dry, barren ground can result from overuse by humans. This is not a natural desert.

WHO NEEDS A DESERT?

Deserts around the world change over time. They shrink when the climate gets naturally wetter and expand when it dries.

In recent decades, desertlike conditions have increased worldwide.

As the human population increases, there is greater demand on land to sustain the crops and livestock that feed us.

Climate change, irrigation, soil erosion, and overgrazing by animals can lead to unnatural deserts through a process called desertification. Cutting down trees for fuel or to increase farmland can create them, too.

When land becomes useless for farming, people and livestock can starve and suffer from disease.

Destroying the desert wipes out homes and food for unique plants and animals.

Who needs a desert? We all do.

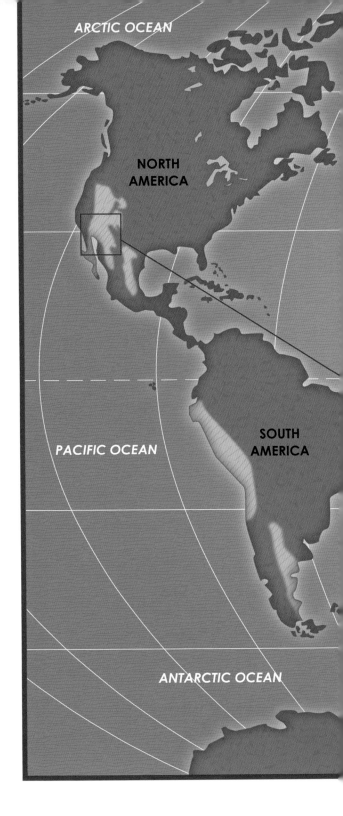

DESERT AREAS OF THE WORLD

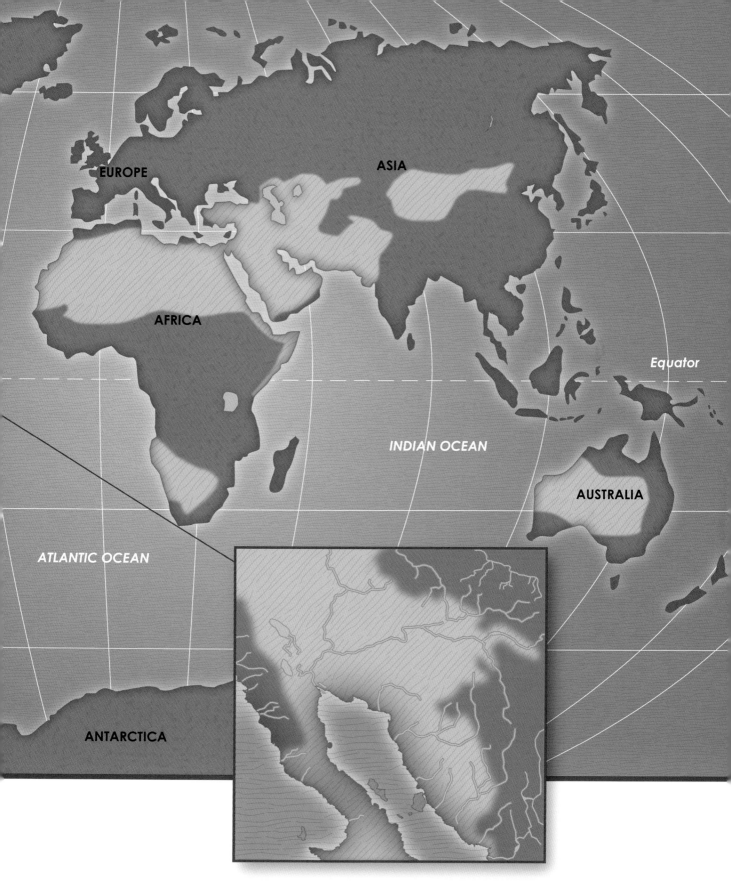

The desert described in this book is in southwestern North America.

HERE IS MORE INFORMATION ABOUT SOME OF THE DESERT INHABITANTS:

Bark Scorpion
Watch out for this scorpion! It has a deadly sting. Because it climbs, it can be found in trees and tall cacti, as well as under rocks and on the ground.

Black-Tailed Jackrabbit
Blood vessels near the surface of its long ears transfer heat to the air and keep the jackrabbit cool. This large hare's young are born covered in fur, their eyes open.

Black Vultures
These scavengers feed on the carcasses of dead animals. They have sharp eyesight and can fly around for hours looking for a meal. Their dark gray heads are featherless.

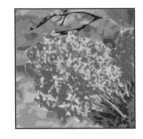

Brittlebush
This plant has a woody trunk, brittle stems, and fuzzy gray-green leaves. Short hairs protect the leaves from cold and heat. The brittlebush is part of the sunflower family.

Coyote
A coyote is an omnivore. It eats almost anything – plants, animals, even insects. It "sings" to communicate with members of its own pack or with other coyotes.

Creosote Bush
New shoots grow from the bush's outer edges, while older stems die in the middle. A ring of bushes branch from the original plant, which can be centuries old.

Desert Holly
The compact shrub's leaves are turned on their edges to protect them from the sun. Its fragrant yellow flowers bloom in spring, and red-orange berries ripen in summer.

Desert Tortoise
This land-dwelling turtle can live for a long time without water or food. Its sturdy feet are not webbed. It cannot swim. If handled, it may empty its bladder in self-defense.

Elf Owl
The elf owl is the world's smallest owl. The female is slightly larger than the male. It nests in a hole in a tree or cactus, already dug out by a woodpecker.

Giant Desert Centipede
This invertebrate has a hard outer casing and a long, multi-sectioned body, with one pair of legs per section. Its bright colors warn of danger. It has a poisonous bite.

Gila Monster
The poisonous Gila monster is a heavy-bodied lizard. It has a short thick tail, where it stores fat for times when food is scarce. It hibernates in winter.

Harris's Hawks
Harris's hawks perch on top of each other's backs, perhaps to get a better view of their hunting area. When the bird on top opens its wings, it shades the one below.

Javelina

The javelina has long, pointed canine teeth. It digs up roots and bulbs with its piglike snout or sharp hooves. Mainly a plant-eater, it also feeds on small dead animals.

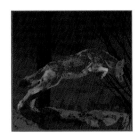

Kit Fox

The kit fox rests in an underground shelter during the day. It gets its water from the blood and moisture of its prey – mainly the kangaroo rat.

Lesser Long-Nosed Bat

Hanging upside down in a cave, this bat spends its day with thousands of others. It feeds only on the fruit and nectar of night-blooming cacti.

Mesquite Tree

This hardy legume tree produces sweet bean pods, which animals eat. People dry and grind the pods into flour. The mesquite's long "taproot" reaches deep into the ground for water.

Mountain Lion

A powerful hunter, the mountain lion sneaks up and ambushes its prey. The big cat kills it quickly, with a bite to the back of the neck or throat.

Palo Verde Tree

Palo verde means "green stick" in Spanish. The tree has small leaves, spine-tipped branches, and green bark. It can live for a hundred years or more.

Prickly Pear Cactus

The wide flat paddles of this cactus are covered with tiny barbed hairs. Clumps of long white spines grow from small bumps, dotting the surface of the paddles.

Ringtail

This nocturnal hunter is a relative of the raccoon. It has excellent eyesight and a keen sense of smell. Its fluffy, black-and-white banded tail is usually longer than its body.

Roadrunner

The largest member of the cuckoo family, the roadrunner would rather run than fly. When feeding its young, liquid trickles from its mouth into its chick's mouth to aid digestion.

Saguaro Cactus

The shallow roots of the saguaro reach out as far as this giant plant is tall. "Saguaro boots" are holes in the cactus that Gila woodpeckers dig out for nests.

Tarantula

The scary-looking spider has a hairy body, eight hairy legs, and eight eyes. It attacks whatever it might be able to eat, such as insects, small lizards, and mice.

Western Diamondback

This poisonous snake is named for the pattern on its skin. Shaking the rattle at the end of its tail, the rattlesnake warns passersby to keep their distance.

GLOSSARY

adapted – changed to suit certain conditions or environments

bacteria – tiny single-celled organisms that break down the remains of other living things

carcasses – the bodies of dead animals

decomposers – organisms that break down dead matter, such as bacteria, fungi, and some types of worms

desert – land that receives an extremely low amount of rain, snow, or hail in a year. Its plants and animals adapt to live in these conditions.

ecosystem – a community of plants, animals, and organisms that interact with each other and their physical environment. There are many different ecosystems on Earth.

environment – the surroundings and conditions in which something exists or lives

erosion – the process of wearing away rock or soil by the action of wind, water, or ice

evaporates – changes from a liquid into a gas or vapor

fertile – capable of producing and nourishing many plants or crops

fungi – nongreen plants, such as mushrooms and molds, which live off other things

inhabitants – living things that dwell in a certain place for a period of time

irrigate – to supply water to a dry area

nocturnal – being active at night

nutrients – substances that give nourishment to a living thing

nutritious – full of nutrients

organic – relating to living matter or what was part of living matter

pollinating – carrying pollen between plants to enable reproduction

prey – an animal that is hunted by another animal for food

springwater – water that rises to the surface from an underground source

topsoil – the upper layer of soil that supplies plants with nourishment

water vapor – tiny water droplets floating in the air

weathering – wearing away by long exposure to wind, rain, and weather